داستان اعداد

THE NUMBER STORY

SMALL BOOK ONE

ENGLISH - PERSIAN

Numbers Teach Children
Their Number Names

written and illustrated by

MISS ANNA

Early Reader Edition of *The Number Story 1*
Bronze Medal Winner, 2016 Wishing Shelf Book Award

Cover by | Lumpy Publishing
Layout by | Lumpy Publishing
Translated by Mozhi
Coloring by Jieeun Woo and Maria Mirabella

Library of Congress Control Number: 2018902040

Names: Miss Anna, author.
Title: Number story : numbers teach children their number names / Miss Anna.
Description: Portland, OR: Lumpy Publishing, 2018.
Identifiers: ISBN 978-1-945977-34-3 | LCCN 2018902040
Summary: The pictures and rhymes present stories which introduce numbers 0-10.
Subjects: LCSH Numeration—English--Persian--Pictorial works--Juvenile literature. | BISAC JUVENILE NONFICTION /
Languages: English--Persian
Classification: LCC QA141.3 .M57 2018 | DDC 513—dc23

Publisher: Lumpy Publishing
Website: www.missannabooks.com
Email: missanna@missannabooks.com

Paperback: ISBN 978-1-945977-34-3
Printed in the U.S.A.   1 3 5 7 9 10 8 6 4 2

Want to learn our number names?

آیا می خواهید نام شماره های ما را بیاموزید؟

It is very easy and a lot of fun!

این بسیار آسان و بسیار سرگرم کننده است!

Say-along our little jingle

ترانه گگ را همرای ما تکرار کنید.

starting from Number One!

از شماره ی یک شروع می کنیم .

1

ONE looks like my one finger.

۱ یک

شبیه انگشت یک من است.

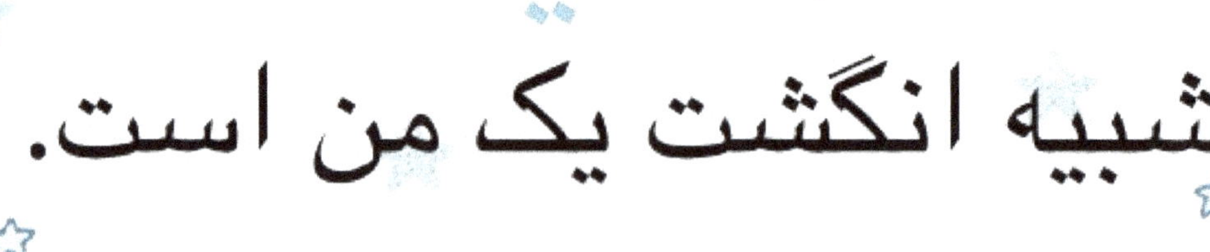

ONE!
يک!

2

TWO trails a tail.

۲ دو

دم را دوست دارد.

A TAIL!   یک دم!

THREE has bumps.

۳ سه

مثل یک تپه است.

BUMPY! ‫تپه ها!‬

4

FOUR carries a sail.

۴ چهار

آن بادبان را حمل می کند.

A SAIL!
یک بادبان!

5

FIVE   is a racing track.

۵ پنج

این مسیر مسابقه ای است.

VROOM

6

SIX   curves like a snail.

۶ ششش

این یک حلزون است.

A SNAIL!   ‏یک حلزون!‏

7

OUCH!
اوه!

8

EIGHT   is rollercoaster rails.

۸ هشت 

آن یک رولر کوستر است.

هورا!
YIPPEE!

9

 is a bubble on a stick.

نه ۹

این یک حباب است.

A BUBBLE!   یک حباب!

10

TEN is an eye of a whale.

۱۰ ده

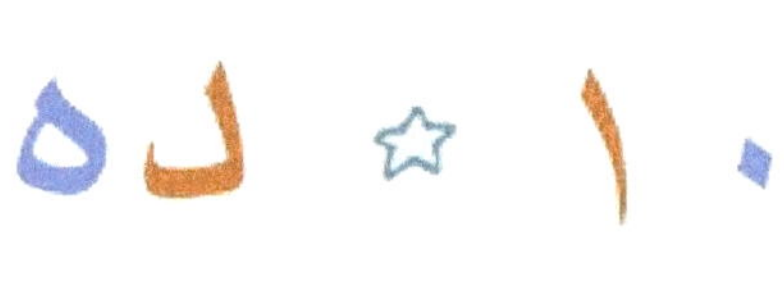

آن یک چشم نهنگ است.

WINK! چشمک!

HELLO! سلام!

And

و

0

ZERO   is an empty pail.

۰ صفر

سطل خالی است.

IT'S EMPTY!
آن خالی است!

Thank you for playing with us today.

We had a lot of fun too!

با تشکر از شما برای بازی امروز با ما.
برای ما نیز خیلی سرگرم کننده بود!

We are your Number friends,
Zero to Ten,
Who will be here for you~

ما دوستان شما هستیم
صفر تا ده
چه کسی برای شما اینجا خواهد بود!

Bye-bye now!
See you again soon.

فعلا خدا حافظ!
به زودی شما را دوباره می بینیم!

The Numbers are *SINGING* too!

To sing-a-long, look for Miss Anna Number Story
at your favorite music store like iTUNES.

MP3

Numbers 0-10
IDENTIFYING
& COUNTING

Numbers 11-20
& Ordinals
first, second, third...

Numbers 0-100
& Place Values
ones, tens, hundreds...

About Clocks
& Telling Time
hours, minutes, seconds...

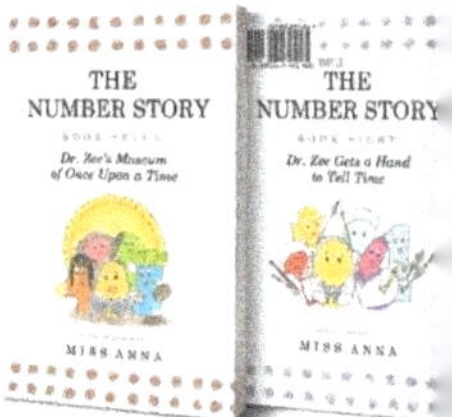

Number Story 1 & 2
isbn: 978-0-996216-48-7

Number Story 3 & 4
isbn: 978-1-945977-01-5

Number Story 5 & 6
isbn: 978-1-945977-06-0

Number Story 7 & 8
isbn: 978-1-949320-40...

For more Miss Anna books to love,
visit us at

www.missannabooks.com

Numbers are working hard all over the world!
Come Travel the World with Us!

9 781945 977343